A Serving of Wisdom

A SERVING OF WISDOM

**Words of
advice and support
for young people**

Kirsty Mooney

SilverWood

Published in 2021 by SilverWood Books

SilverWood Books Ltd
14 Small Street, Bristol, BS1 1DE, United Kingdom
www.silverwoodbooks.co.uk

ISBN 978-1-80042-068-7 (paperback)

British Library Cataloguing in Publication Data
A CIP catalogue record for this book is
available from the British Library

Page design and typesetting by SilverWood Books

For my beautiful Jack and Keira,

Close your eyes and allow me to wrap my arms around you,

I will always be there to hold you,

Love always.

Mum xxx

Contents

Introduction

Young people have a tough time nowadays. For many complex reasons, they are suffering from more mental illness than ever before. As a mother of two teenagers, I am never more aware of this than now and I really believe they need all the help, love and support we adults can provide as they head out into the world. So, in the hope that I could perhaps save my children just a little bit of heartache as they try to negotiate their way over, around or through life's inevitable hurdles, I decided to record some of the wisdom and knowledge I have gained throughout my own life. I also invited my close family and friends to offer some advice. What words of wisdom would they give to my children as they head out into the world? I didn't stop there. In order to encourage some home cooking once the nest has been flown, I invited them all to provide a much-loved family recipe.

Thus, from my early thoughts, *A Serving of Wisdom* slowly emerged into a unique gift for a young person who is beginning their journey into the wider world. It's not just a gift from my heart but a gift from many hearts. My hope is that this simple serving of wisdom offers young people a little bit of peace of mind as they embark upon their own journey. In two parts, the book firstly covers anecdotes from my life experiences and the wisdom and knowledge I have gained along the way. Themes include the importance of having a strong support network, relationships, health and well-being, and problem-solving, as well as exploring attitude and confidence.

Part two offers some wonderful words from my friends and family along with a selection of delicious recipes to set you on your way.

If you are giving this book to a young person as a gift, I have left space on the next page for you to add your own serving of wisdom.

I hope you enjoy it.

Kirsty Mooney

P.S. The profits from this book will be donated to young people's charities.

A serving of wisdom from

....
....

My words of wisdom for you are

....
....
....
....

Our favourite family recipe is

....
....
....
....
....
....
....
....
....
....
....
....
....
....

Part 1

A Serving of Wisdom from Me

Family and Friends

One of the most important things in life is family. They are your foundation, your bricks and mortar. Whether you like it or not, they instil a set of values in you and play a major role in helping you to develop your identity. They play a big part in who you are. Having said that, parents can only go so far in terms of raising you, the rest is up to you.

Family should be there for you through the highs and lows – to love and support you, to celebrate with you, to commiserate with you, to boost you up, to ground you and to forgive you. Of course, it's not always the case that families are able to be loving and caring – it depends so much on their own experiences and circumstances, but wouldn't the world be a much better place if we all had a loving and caring family and a safe place to call home?

We can all be guilty of taking our families for granted and thinking they will always be around, but the truth is that life is short, and we never really know what is coming round the corner, so really understanding the importance of family might perhaps help you to cherish and appreciate them.

When I left home to go to university, I could not wait to get away and have my independence. I had the cigarettes out before my mum and dad had got to the end of the street. I had tried everything by the end of the second week of term and had run out of money by the fourth week. By week six I had finally started to settle down and began to feel quite homesick, realising that a good home-cooked meal and some TLC from Mum and Dad would be very gratefully received.

As parents we know you are desperate to leave home but spare a thought for how we feel when you leave. Make your transition a happy and loving one, and for heaven's sake, stay in touch.

Families are not just made of our own flesh and blood. We create families throughout our lives – groups of people who make us happy and who give us the love and support we need. A few years ago, I attended the funeral of a close friend. It was an incredible occasion, full of sadness but also full of joy and laughter in celebration of the person he was. Before he died, he had written a letter which was to be read out at his funeral. In the letter he talked of his Irish family (his blood relations), his German family (his wife's family), his Scottish family (us), and so it went on describing five or six 'families' who had all been a huge part of his life. What a great way to describe family.

Our friends are equally important and complement our family.

We tend to gravitate towards people who have similar values to us. The characteristics we like about ourselves we look for in others. It's natural.

My own friendship circle consists of a small group of people with whom I have a lot in common. We get on well, have similar interests and really respect and trust each other to say it how it is. However, there is nothing better than being with someone who is the exact opposite of you because they will allow you to see the world through different eyes. One of my friends is a bit 'hippy', is very creative and has had different life experiences from me. I love her for who she is and her take on the world. Another friend of mine is never afraid to speak her mind and manages to do so in the most articulate way, irrespective of the situation. She's bold and funny. We are all different. So, it's interesting to open ourselves up to the possibility of other points of view, other ideas and other ways of being in the world – that helps us to learn and to grow.

How boring would it be if we only listened to people who are the same as us?

Sometimes friendships can become really hard work and just downright painful. We find ourselves wondering why we are continuing with this drudgery. Perhaps it is time to reassess your relationship with that person. Do they radiate beautiful, infectious energy or do they drain you of energy, leaving you feeling negative and irritable? Do they ask how you are or is it all about them? Do you find it hard to know how to take what they say because they are full of passive aggressive comments and tiny amounts of sarcasm? I had a friend who would always find a way to make fun of me in other people's company. Her comments were cleverly balanced between making her audience laugh and making a fool of me. In other words, all the jokes were at my expense. Of course, we all need a sense of humour and to be able to laugh at ourselves. However, if it feels like you are always the butt of the joke then it would be a good idea to examine the basis for that particular friendship. You don't even need to call it out if that feels too uncomfortable. You could just vote with your feet and gently ease yourself away.

Reassess who you really want to spend your time with as opposed to who you think you should be spending your time with. Spend your valuable time with people who will help you to shine.

"Friendship is a single soul dwelling in two bodies."

Aristotle

Your Support Network

My old dad used to say, "No man is an island." He had good reason to say that to me as I was the ultimate example of an island (and still can be). I would not share how I was feeling, preferring to live inside my head. Nothing good comes of this and the risk is that we end up isolated, lonely and a bit depressed.

We are not built to do life on our own.

I wish I had listened to my old dad then.

So, on that note, one of the most important things we can have in our lives is a strong support network. What do I mean by that? A group of people in your life you can depend on to be there for you – no matter what. A circle of people you will listen to and trust. Each person in your network will be there for a different reason. They will all provide you with something unique because they are unique. For example, one might tell you something you really don't want to hear, or another might have great advice about a work problem. Hopefully, there will be a few in your network who are strictly for fun only! They will all be different, and you will all share your experiences and support each other.

I mean this in the nicest possible way but *use* your network to support you whenever you feel you need it – you really can't do life on your own.

Relationships

Positive, healthy relationships are important for our well-being and one of the key measurements of our happiness. They are about mutual respect and feeling valued, safe and supported. It is natural to have good times and challenging times, but it is not natural to be in a relationship with someone who continually makes you feel bad about yourself.

> *"No relationship is ever worth sacrificing your dignity or self-respect for."*
>
> Anonymous

The most unsuccessful relationships I've had have been where I have not been true to myself. It is important to accept yourself as you are, not who someone wants you to be. In positive, healthy relationships you will be loved for being you and all that goes with you. Don't ever apologise for being you.

> *"The greatest happiness of life is the conviction that we are loved; loved for ourselves, or rather, loved in spite of ourselves."*
>
> Victor Hugo

Relationships break down for all sorts of reasons. For one, we can all at times find it hard to accept people just as they are. We think everyone should be like us, have our values and adopt our point of view, and if they don't, we judge them.

If you can accept people and situations just as they are, you will be a lot happier. We do not have the power to change people and they do not have the power to change us. Of course, it is easy to be influenced by what people say and do, but the only minds we can change are our own. Please don't waste your energy on trying to do the impossible – it's exhausting! Wouldn't you like people to take you just as you are?

"I love you for who you are, not what you do, how you behave, what you achieve or what you look like."

Anonymous

Another cause of relationship difficulty is poor communication: not telling people how we feel and what we want. How else can our needs be met if we are not honest with people? The danger is we become unfulfilled, leading to resentment, frustration, anxiety, anger and a whole heap of other negative emotions. Ask yourself this, "If I speak up and ask for my needs to be met, what is the worst that can happen?" The world won't fall apart because you have asked someone for something you want. At least you have taken that first giant step. There is no shame in it, and it's not selfish or rude. It is simply asking for your needs to be met. Why do we find this so difficult and uncomfortable? Do we not deserve to have our needs met? Are we not worthy of this? We would want our family or our best friends' needs to be met, so why not ours? People can't second guess you – they don't know what you are thinking, so tell them, no matter how uncomfortable it feels at the time. You will feel so empowered, I promise. I wish someone had told me that when I was growing up. We can spend an awful lot of time trying to guess what someone is thinking – and be totally wrong. Just think of all that wasted energy.

It's also all about *how* you ask. If you go about demanding what you want and jumping up and down, you are more likely to cause irritation. If what you say is well thought through you will be more likely to succeed. Try writing down what it is you want to say first and practise in the mirror until you are comfortable with saying it. This way you will be able to craft what it is you want to say and filter out the stuff that is not useful. It takes practise but if you can develop this skill you are more likely to feel more confident and in control.

These conversations can be challenging and uncomfortable but don't be afraid to have them just because you will be out of your comfort zone. These are the ones that will help you to develop your emotional skills.

Be brave, speak out. Ask for what you want.

Of course, there is a flip side to this and that is being able to listen to the other person. A real sign of maturity is to be prepared to *really* find out what the other person is thinking.

Can you put yourself in their shoes and see the world from their point of view? Can you reflect what they are telling you? This ability to empathise with someone will help you to become a much-valued friend and confidante.

Everyone comes into our lives for a reason and they will all teach us something and bring out aspects of ourselves we have not explored yet. All these lessons will serve us well and help us to grow. The dating game has radically changed since I was young. It seems more relaxed and casual now. That being said, what we feel for a person is still at the centre of how we will treat them.

As a young woman, I had a few stormy relationships. I would be in a relationship with someone, we'd split up, we'd get back together, we'd split up again, we'd get back together and so it would go around in circles. I was unhappy, stressed and continually anxious, and that is no way to live. In the meantime, all my friends were in strong, stable relationships. I finally confided in a good friend and asked her why she thought this was always happening to me. Sometimes we really need our friends to be blunt with us, and thankfully she was. She told me that I was repeating the same mistakes and not learning from them. I was falling into the same trap and had turned it into a habit. I realised that the two previous relationships I'd had were just repeats of the same issues but with different people. *Both* partners had very dominant personalities, so the relationships never felt equal or balanced and that is not a good formula for someone with fairly low self-esteem in the first place. No wonder the outcome was always the same. Deep down, I knew all this, but I had chosen to turn a blind eye to the fact that these relationships were not for me. I really believe that the universe will present us with the same problem (but in a different guise) until we recognise that something needs to change.

Feeling rather bruised and battered, I finally found the courage not to allow history to repeat itself for a third time, so I chose a different path. It was not an easy choice; it took great courage and determination, but it was the best thing I ever did. I emerged stronger, more empowered and much happier. When I finally met my husband, I saw a good man – kind, funny, loyal, caring, passionate, loving and determined. He was worth the lessons I had to learn in order to find him, so don't compromise on finding the right partner – it'll never work if you do.

If you ever need a reminder of how not to repeat the same mistakes, take a look at a wonderful poem by Portia Nelson called 'There's a Hole in my Sidewalk: The Romance of Self-Discovery'. It will tell you all you need to know.

Love makes us grow and we need it to survive. Allow yourself to be loved and cherished — there is no greater feeling than the ability to give and receive love.

Gratitude

No matter how awful my day has been I try to find something to be grateful for. A beautiful sunny day, finding a parking space, not burning the dinner! You will always be able to find something to be grateful for, even in your darkest moments – and I hope you don't have too many of those.

Gratitude is a wonderful thing to get into the habit of practising because it can put things into perspective. If we go through our lives without expressing or feeling gratitude, we will jaundice our view of the world. It becomes a place where we only take and don't give back. Gratitude is how we really appreciate what we have. My niece told me about a technique she uses at bedtime. She thinks about the 'peak' of her day and the 'lesson' of her day – the peak being the highlight or best part of her day and the lesson something she could have done differently. This is also a really nice way to show yourself some compassion.

Another way of feeling grateful is to do something that is a real leveller. By that I mean do something that brings you right back down to earth and makes you realise just how lucky you are. It could be as simple as walking along the street and realising that you are healthy and fit compared to some people or that you have a roof over your head. All these things can put your life into perspective and make you feel grateful for the life you have. It can also have a positive effect on your mental health.

> *"It is not the happiness that brings us gratitude. It is the gratitude that brings us happiness."*
>
> Anonymous

Celebrations

"Our memories are the only paradise from which we can never be expelled."

Jean Paul Richter

It is so important to celebrate. I get the champagne (or more like the cava) out at every opportunity. Birthdays, new jobs, meeting a friend, anniversaries, New Year or just because it's Friday (or even Tuesday). It is important to mark a moment as it helps us celebrate what we have. It is the physical manifestation of gratitude. Even if there is nothing official to celebrate, find something. It is genuinely good for your well-being, so make some memories and fill your life with people that make you sparkle and shine. It will make such a difference to your life. If you do find that you have overindulged (heaven forbid), then my go-to cure is a bowl of fresh fruit and several cups of green tea. Failing that – a Bloody Mary!

I know you probably think that life will go on forever, but it won't. Life is short. Please don't waste time thinking about the past or dreaming that life will be better tomorrow. Live every single moment in the here and the now – be present. It is the only place that matters.

My old dad (yes, him again) used to say, "Go and enjoy yourself… but not too much!" Although it was said fairly tongue in cheek and with a glint in his eye, there was a lot of that old Scottish Presbyterian in him saying don't have *too* good a time.

Sorry, Dad, but…stuff that… Go and have an absolute ball!!!!

Kindness

"Three things in human life are important. The first is to be kind. The second is to be kind. And the third is to be kind."

Henry James

When we are journeying through our youth, we are probably not the kindest of people. We only think of ourselves and we don't usually appreciate the wider universe. We are self-centred and can be a pain in the ass. Hopefully, as we grow into adulthood, our ego takes a back seat as kindness and compassion come to the fore.

For me, kindness is one of the most wonderful qualities a person can have. We can't always remember what someone said but we sure as heck will remember how they made us feel. Every single person on this planet matters. As I write, we are going through a period where there is a terrible lack of kindness in our society. This is partly fuelled by the fact that people think they can say anything they like on social media and get away with it. We are also a less tolerant society, more insular and more complex, so it's up to us to step up our acts of kindness. Beat them, don't join them. It is incredible how one simple act of kindness can make someone's day and make their world a bit better. I know how I feel when someone does something nice for me – it makes me feel like I matter. Believe it or not, kindness is also contagious – if we witness or receive an act of kindness, we are more likely to be kind to someone else. It has been scientifically proven to improve happiness.

I remember not being kind to someone. I was working hard, stressed and not very happy in myself. I was travelling home from New York having worked there for a week. This was in the days when we checked our bags in on the pavement outside the terminal. Can you imagine doing that now? Anyway, this older woman with big suitcases bustled up to the front of the queue I had patiently been waiting in for ages. Before I could stop myself, I sent her right to the back of the queue – I didn't even give her a chance to explain. Although in the grand scheme of things this wasn't a terrible *unkindness*, it was a turning point for me and demonstrated that I needed to change. I didn't like the person I had become as I had shown no kindness or compassion whatsoever.

I resigned from my job the following week.

The chairman of a large company I worked for was a very clever businessman. He was on the board of several organisations and had grown them into very prosperous companies. He understood what made people tick and he got the best out of them. He had the amazing ability to balance the running of a large and successful business with being a human being. He was compassionate, empathic and kind.

I kept in touch with him for many years after I left the organisation, and he would often tell me that a really good life is created by giving, not getting.

> "Getting money is not all a man's business: to cultivate kindness is a valuable part of the business of life."
>
> Samuel Johnson

Practising kindness is not about simply doing the right thing. Be kind because you want to be kind — it will make you happy.

Just one final word: it is also important to be kind to ourselves.

Problem-solving

"When one door closes, another opens; but we often look so long and so regretfully upon the closed door that we do not see the one which has opened for us."

Alexander Graham Bell

I believe that we will strengthen our resilience if we can learn to solve our own problems. If we have a greater ability to bounce back it will give us a more optimistic outlook on life because we know that whatever life throws at us, we will be able to deal with it. Young people need to be taught how to overcome setbacks and deal positively with failure. Many academics and businesses understand that failure is more important than success because we can learn from our mistakes. There are now 'failure academies' which exist solely to understand failure so that we can learn how to move forward and have greater success.

I know that it is easy to say, but if we let our problems drag us down, we will find it harder to get back up. I honestly believe that only we can solve our own problems. We cannot rely on someone else to sort them out for us. Of course, our support network and our peers can help, but we are responsible for ourselves and we have to try. If we approach our problems with an element of hope and a belief that things will get better (optimism), we will find a way through. If you learn to overcome setbacks and smash through barriers, you will thrive in ways you can only imagine.

I would first like to share an extract from a letter that I wrote a few years ago to my younger self. I often look at it as it reminds me that no matter what, I can get through life's challenges.

"I would like to tell you that you have some wonderful tools to help you grow and nurture your soul. You are worthwhile; you are important; you are as good as everyone else. Over the years your soul can get pushed, shoved, battered and bruised – it might get shamed, rejected and controlled or made to feel unworthy. Well, I am here to tell you that whatever challenges are presented to you, I am here to hold your hand and together we will learn to nurture and nourish your soul."

Here are a few of my suggestions to help you to develop your problem-solving skills:

✓ Can you get the problem into perspective? Try pretending that you are in a helicopter a thousand feet above the ground. How big is this problem? Is it life or death? This is a great way to really find out the size of a problem and to try to make sense of it. You might find that it is not as overwhelming as you thought.

✓ Ask yourself, "What is the worst that can happen?" Again, this is a way of putting the problem into perspective.

✓ Who can help me with this? Ask for help. There is absolutely no shame in asking for help. It is a sign of strength. Remember your network? That is what it's for. Literally ask yourself, "Who might be able to help me to work through this problem?"

✓ If you find yourself obsessing about a problem, then go and do something else to distract yourself and come back to it when you are more refreshed. You might find that you are more able to take a whole new approach to it. You could also set aside some 'worrying time' every day – ten or fifteen minutes to devote constructive time to your problem. This might help you remove the feelings of obsession.

✓ Use your breath. Fill your body up with nice, positive energy and expel the old energy that might be stopping you from seeing clearly. Even a minute of slow, deliberate breathing can make all the difference.

✓ Can the problem be broken into small, manageable pieces? What part of this problem can I control? What part can I not control and therefore put to one side? This might help you to focus on what you can change.

✓ Write down the pros and cons of the problem and weigh each one up. Take a view on each one in terms of what you can do about it. Can someone help you with it? Write down possible solutions.

✓ Can you try to *trust* that the situation will be resolved and that the best outcome will present itself? I have lost count of the number of times I have had a problem and finally given in to simply 'trusting' that it will all work out in the end. As my mum used to say, "Have a little faith." You might be surprised at the outcome.

✓ Finally, if you really don't know which direction to take then ask yourself how it would feel to choose one and run with it, because doing something might be better than being stagnant and doing nothing at all.

Sometimes you will have to dig very deep to get out of whatever is going on but never, ever doubt that you have enough inside you to help you to deal with it. You will always find a way through. *We are only given the challenges that the universe knows we will have the ability to cope with. Believe that you can get through whatever life throws at you.*

And never, ever, ever, ever, ever give up.

Just a quick word on being 'stuck'. This is something that has happened to me several times throughout my life. It is a position where your energy is so stagnant that you are unable to move forward, backwards or even sideways and just cannot see a way through. You literally do not know what to do. There is an overwhelming feeling of being powerless and helpless.

Whenever this has happened to me, I have had the urge to use my energy until I'm exhausted – going for a run, a cycle, a walk in the hills, punch a pillow – anything that has got me really out of breath. That stagnant energy needs to move, and brisk exercise is one way to do it. Secondly, never more than at the point where I am stuck have I had the need to scream very loudly until whatever is locked inside gets out; even screaming into a pillow will help. Just don't keep it inside – you will go mad!

There are also some wonderful and highly effective therapies to help you shift blocked energy. The therapies I am most familiar with are shiatsu, reiki and acupuncture, though there are many, many more. Our mind, body and soul work best when our energy is flowing freely.

The following quote is from Ancient Greek times and was written by Arrian, a student of the Greek philosopher Epictetus:

> *"It's not what happens to you, but how you react to it that matters. When something happens, the only thing in your power is your attitude towards it; you can either accept it or resent it."*

Health and Well-being

Many young people today are experiencing mental health issues. They are suffering from a range of problems from anxiety, depression and panic attacks to ongoing low moods. It is a desperately worrying trend and it makes me so sad to see young people suffering like this when they should be enjoying life. How has this happened? I am not qualified to provide a professional explanation for this however I can see for myself that young people are under unbearable pressure. They want to do well in exams in a climate of league tables that can leave them feeling that they are not good enough. They live in their own world of social media which is not always healthy. They are taking low-paid jobs that do not match their skillsets, and probably have money worries that may have arisen from student loans or zero-hours contracts. All of this is having a very damaging effect on their mental well-being. Who wouldn't suffer with all that stress? It would send even the most resilient of adults into freefall.

Nowadays, we have over-stimulated minds. My mum used to tell me that I would get square eyes from watching too much television. She worried that I would turn into a zombie! I wonder what she would make of our media habits today. She would be spinning in her grave. Who would have thought that our excessive media habits could contribute to migraines, anxiety, depression? And yet that is exactly what we are facing. We rarely look up from our phones and our phones are rarely off. If we're not on a phone then we're on a laptop, a desktop, an iPad, an Xbox etc. We literally never switch off. All this *stuff* can stop us feeling and put us in danger of living on autopilot. The irony is that we are living in an acutely connected world and my sense is we are becoming more disconnected and emotionally isolated than ever. Our brains must rest to grow. We must allow our minds to have some downtime. How can we allow the time to work out what is wrong with us when we are unable to rest our minds? We are not giving ourselves any space – no wonder we are suffering.

Lack of self-nourishment and self-care could lead to depression.

I have gone through a few periods of depression in my life and I think they were caused by trying to battle on rather than stopping and asking for help. I had got used to the idea that I was fine, but I wasn't – not by a long way. Perhaps a build-up of many things – exhaustion from coping with two small children, loss of sense of myself and grieving for my mum who was in a care home and suffering from dementia.

I wrote the following verse when I could feel that I was sinking into the depths of despair.

Where Have I Gone?

I look in the mirror and what do I see?
A blank and motionless face
Staring back at me
Joyless eyes that no longer shine
A tight mouth, a straight line.
Where have I gone?
What has happened to me?
Aha – my old friend, the Black Dog
Has crept up on me.
A gradual slide – something not quite right
Once it starts it's hard to stop
Strong, like a powerful magnet
Pulling me in
My heart sinking

A giant anvil sitting on my chest
It's hard to breathe
I am disconnecting.

It's done – I have closed down.
Surrounded by the bell jar
Trapped in my self

So what now?
The landscape is flat
Such a familiar sight.

It's not the first time
And it will not be the last.
So, I will wait it out.

My one thought?
This will pass
This will pass
This will pass.

I have always found it hard to ask for help, but in the midst of one particularly awful period I finally decided to seek assistance and found a wonderful psychotherapist. It was the best thing I ever did, so if you have feelings like this, please, please seek help.

Here are some suggestions that might help you:

Stop and take the time to check in with yourself. How do you feel? Can you describe it? Can you function on a daily basis? Do you feel happy most of the time? Do you feel sad most of the time? Try to separate what are normal feelings (happy, angry, sad etc.) from feelings that are more concerning and may last longer than you think they should. It is an impossibility and is not normal to feel happy all the time but nor is it normal to be feeling low, unhappy or angry all the time. If you are like this then please talk to someone so that you can start to seek help.

Listen to what your body is telling you. The body and mind are inextricably linked, which means that whatever is going on in your mind will appear at some point in your body. It is worth paying attention to what is going on. Take a good look at yourself. What are your eyes like? Are they clear, dull, empty? Is your tongue nice and clean or is it dirty? How is your tummy? Does it ache? Is it bloated, empty? Do you feel sick all the time? Your body provides lots of clues to what is going on and it will soon tell you that enough is enough and that it is time to deal with your feelings. Bottling up your feelings is storing up problems for the future. As a shiatsu practitioner, I am a great believer in alternative therapies. Don't underestimate the power of a wonderful touch and/or talking therapist.

Be kind to yourself. Do you think you could try to treat yourself with the same kindness as you would your best pal? This seems to be a really hard thing to do – are you not worthy? Do you think that love and kindness is for other people, only to be dished out and not taken in? Why do we reserve kindness only for other people? Find some lovely nurturing activities to make you feel good.

Breathe. I cannot stress enough the importance of using your breath. When we are stressed or upset, we can get short of breath and feel tight-chested. The chances are we are not thinking straight. STOP. Try to ground yourself. The way I do this is by sitting down for a few minutes with my feet flat on the ground. I close my eyes and take a deep breath in through my nose and then slowly breathe out through my mouth. I do this for three or four minutes to just get me to feel calm. Your breathing will become steadier and your heart rate will begin to slow down. Imagine that your energy is going down through the soles of your feet and deep into the earth. You will hopefully start to feel a sense of calm. This can be done anywhere, whether in an exam or on the bus. Just feel into it.

Another popular breathing technique is called the 'four square breath'. This is so easy to do and can be done anywhere:

✓ Slowly breathe in through your nose for a slow count of four.

✓ Hold your breath for a count of four.

✓ Breathe out through your mouth for a count of four.

✓ Hold your breath gently for a count of four.

✓ Repeat as often as you like.

Flow. Can you try to go with the flow? This is so much easier said than done and I must admit that I have spent many times swimming against the tide – it's utterly exhausting. So, try not to let the small things bug you; let them go. If you miss a bus, get the next one. If someone is really irritating you, walk away. I am envious of people who go with the flow; they are more easy-going, so it's worth a try. Practise on something small and see how you get on. Then try it again and keep practising it until it becomes second nature. Some people can embrace change and get very excited about it. Others have to be dragged kicking and screaming along the way. Can you imagine how stressful that must be when the alternative is so much easier? If you are that person, ask yourself, "Why? Why am I so reluctant for change?" Usually, it will have something to do with fear – fear of failure.

Exercise. Taking regular exercise releases happy hormones which helps to boost your mood. It can also help you to sleep better and to feel more energetic. It is such a powerful antidote for depression, anxiety, stress and more.

Fresh air. Get out into the fresh air – please! Some sunshine or wind or rain on your face will make you feel better and help to get rid of stagnant energy.

Diet. There is no doubt about it: you are what you eat, and a poor diet can lead to all sorts of problems from skin breakouts, obesity, depression, low mood and high blood pressure. What we put into our gut matters. The health of our gut reflects our overall health and well-being. I don't think we need to be totally obsessive about it, just mindful about how we are looking after our gut. If you are living on a diet of junk food and energy drinks, then it is very likely you will not feel well in yourself. If you balance your diet with fruit, vegetables, water, pulses and grains, fish and meat then the chances are you will feel healthier. Try to cook instead of buying ready meals. All the meals in this book are cooked from scratch. Get a few basic meals in your repertoire that will keep you healthy and interested in food.

Sleep. It's a no-brainer that a good night's sleep will make a difference to your day. Turn your phone off – don't keep it under your pillow. An uninterrupted night is so good for you. Your mind will rest, and your brain will get the chance to grow as you sleep. Your mood will improve, and you will be more able to put into proportion and face any challenges that come your way. Have you ever tried to sort out a problem when you have been overtired? It's practically impossible to think clearly.

Talk. Remember that support network I mentioned earlier? Well, this is where it comes into its own. Talk. Tell someone in your trusted network if you are feeling rubbish.

Express yourself. Find different ways to express yourself – dance, sing, laugh, write letters to yourself, meditate, talk to an imaginary recipient. Find a way to let it all out. You will be amazed at the result.

Distraction. If you find yourself getting stuck in your head and obsessing about the same things and unable to move forward, try some distraction techniques. If you are sitting down then move to another seat, go for a run, go for a walk, do some cooking, phone a friend – anything not to be going over the same old stuff again and again in your head; it's not helpful.

Mindfulness meditation. This is a wonderful way to help you to reconnect with yourself and be totally present. There are so many benefits to mindfulness, from boosting your mood to strengthening your immune system and reducing anxiety, stress and depression.

One thing I have learned is that I am most content when the various aspects of my life are in balance. My relationships are stable and positive, I feel mentally and physically well, and my life has some meaning. I think I am doing well if I can achieve about seventy-five per cent of this mix. Perfection is impossible but balance is not. Unless you are an enlightened monk, delirious happiness is not achievable. Contentment, however, is achievable and much more sustainable long-term.

Contentment is the new black.

Forgiveness and Letting Go

I have clung on to things all my life. I have cupboards full of clothes and old shoes, old bits of jewellery, old books – you name it and I still have it. I can also cling on to unhelpful thought patterns and allow these to hold me back. Nowadays, social media means we hold on to even more stuff because once it's out there we can't bring it back. This results in our actions and our opinions being embedded in the digital universe forever, meaning there will always be someone to remind you of something that you may not be proud of. How, then, can we learn to let all that go so that we live mentally healthy lives? It sounds too simple, but we have a choice to make. We either hold on to stuff and allow it to twist us up and make us unwell or we let it go and move on. The more we carry on our shoulders, the sorer our backs will be. Memories, incidents, events that you'd rather forget will always arise, but we need to be kind to ourselves and ask some questions, "Do these memories serve me well? Do they help me to live a happy life?" If both answers are no, then we must *choose* to let them go. Distraction is key. When these thoughts and memories come into our minds, acknowledge that they are there and then actively choose to think about something else. Our minds will always play tricks, so we need to have lots of tools in our kit so that the negative stuff does not take over.

You will make mistakes; you will mess up; you will do something stupid, something thoughtless or something embarrassing.

That is part of life and no one is perfect. STOP. To dwell on these things will project your mind into turmoil. When my mind is in turmoil, I feel physically unwell and my heart starts racing, and believe me, at my age I can't afford to have a racing heart! It is understandable to feel guilty about something, but please do not torture yourself and continue to beat yourself up over some silly mistake. That is destructive. You are only human. Learn to forgive yourself and move on. This is where breathing techniques are really useful to help calm your mind.

There will always be people around who will remind you of your shortcomings, but ask yourself a simple question, "Do you want them to be in your life?" There will also be people in your life who will never forgive you for something that was said or that happened years ago. That is up to them. Try not to get drawn into it. Take the moral high ground. What kind of person would you like to be, forgiving or shackled with all the unpleasant energy that goes hand in hand with a lack of forgiveness?

Forgiveness sets you free to enjoy your life, to feel lighter and happier. Have some compassion for the people who will not forgive you because they are on their own journey but try to leave them behind.

"Forgotten is forgiven."

F. Scott Fitzgerald

Again, mindfulness meditation is a wonderful technique for quietening our noisy minds and calming our thoughts. Please, please try not to let these unhelpful thoughts win. They will never serve you well.

Jobs and Careers

The jobs market is so different nowadays. It is much more challenging, complex and diverse. Young people have two or three jobs, and they are very rarely jobs that match their wonderful capabilities or indeed value them as individuals. Low-paid or zero-hours contracts are endemic, resulting in young people being unable to plan their lives or get out of the poverty trap. That must be so stressful.

When I was a young woman, I was trying to develop my career in a very male-dominated business world. Although I was good at my job, it wasn't until years later when I was reflecting on my career that I realised that I had been in the wrong career all along. I had followed my friends into business instead of following my heart and doing something that would have reflected the very essence of me. No wonder I found it so challenging; I was too sensitive for that cut-throat world and I was pushing water uphill all the time. Don't feel too sorry for me: I was well paid and got to see a lot of the world. However, I doubt that I was really being myself the entire time and that takes a huge emotional toll. So, what's my message? Find something you want to do that comes from your heart. Play to your strengths, ask yourself (or someone else) what your unique strengths and qualities are. Don't follow your pal. Ask yourself, "What did I want to be when I was a child?" Children are so honest, open and clear about things. I know that some of the answers will be a bus driver, fireman, doctor etc. as these are the typecasts that children still play with. However, if your ambition then was to be a doctor but academically that is totally out of reach for you, perhaps the message is that you should be in some sort of caring profession that reflects your very essence. Not following your pals brings other benefits too – it means you can continually reinvent yourself. I love that idea.

There will always be jobs that you're not keen on and these may well be necessary to pay the bills but strive to find something that reflects you and that you enjoy. It will make getting up in the morning much easier, believe me.

The one thing I wish I'd had when I was working was a good mentor, someone I could go to for advice and support. If you work with someone you really like who is in a more senior role, don't be afraid to ask them if they will mentor you. Remember, what's the worst that can happen? They can only say no.

Another great piece of advice I got was to surround myself with experts – learn from others. That will help you to grow your professional network.

Whatever your grand plan is, try to have a plan B as well. This does not mean you are being pessimistic or thinking you might fail; it is a sign of common sense and an optimistic outlook on life. If something goes wrong, you are prepared. That reassurance will give you confidence and will stop you being ground down by adversity.

A final word: invest in yourself.

Whether it be your health, your well-being, a decent haircut, an idea, your education, your own journey of self-discovery – invest. If you don't, why should anyone else? Try to be the best version of yourself that you can be. This will build your confidence, your self-worth, and most importantly, insure you against selling yourself short.

The Importance of Attitude

"The real secret to success is enthusiasm."

Walter Chrysler

Three things that have not changed in the world of work are the importance of showing an employer you are willing to work hard, a positive 'can do anything' attitude and bags of initiative.

Strive to stand out from the crowd.

Ask lots of questions. Some of the most successful people are those who have challenged the norm. They are inquisitive and they want to find ways to improve things. That kind of attitude will get you noticed.

I mentioned earlier that I was in the wrong job and as a consequence of that my attitude wasn't always great. I remember sitting in a large meeting to hear the results of some research the company had undertaken. The meeting lasted hours and I was bored stiff doodling on my pad. After the meeting one of the sales managers came over to me and told me if I worked for him, he would sack me on the spot because my attitude stank. Ouch. That really hurt. Sometimes it takes an outsider to point out our shortcomings. However, the bigger picture was that perhaps I should have realised then that I was in the wrong job. I worked in the same profession for another fifteen years, though I did improve my attitude!

Get Out of Your Comfort Zone

Be brave. Have courage.

"Use your fear...it can take you to the place where you store your courage."

Amelia Earhart

Do you remember the first time you went without stabilisers? Your first day at high school? Your first exam? Your first trip on a bus by yourself? Your first date? I remember when I went to university. I had been surrounded by my own type of friends throughout school and suddenly I was propelled into meeting people from all different walks of life, with different backgrounds and different points of view. I had naively thought that everyone was like me. Well, you would at seventeen. That was quite a learning curve and both exciting and terrifying in equal measure. Each one of these firsts was a new challenge and involved stepping well out of my comfort zone.

Everyone has times when they feel like crawling under a rock or sneaking away before anyone see us – I know I do. We are afraid of making a fool of ourselves, scared we'll get laughed at and scared that we will fail. All these negative emotions stir around in our stomachs. No wonder we can start to feel a bit sick. The one overriding emotion associated with failure is shame.

However, and here's the rub, no-one has ever grown whilst sitting on their backside – you have to try. Don't be afraid to try something new or something that you think is slightly beyond your capabilities. What

43

is the worst that can happen? Some level of discomfort is good for you. It gets the adrenalin going. Your critical inner voice serves no purpose whatsoever and will only ever hold you back, so replace it with nicer, kinder thoughts. You have sole charge of your mind so you can choose to have kind and encouraging thoughts, or you can choose to have critical thoughts.

"You can do anything you decide to do."

Amelia Earhart

That brings me on to my second point: mistakes are good. Making a mistake is how we learn. Don't ever be embarrassed when you make a mistake, and don't be too afraid to try something new for fear of making a mistake. The truth is that if you don't try, you will never know. I used to take it all far too seriously and be far too hard on myself, so try to just laugh it off if you make a mistake. It is not the end of the world. The healthiest people I know are the ones who laugh a lot and are not afraid to laugh at themselves. If possible, seek out people to help and support you who are kind, non-judgemental – and who laugh.

Over time, you will become more courageous and more confident. What a great feeling!

I am a huge believer in celebrating success. Once you have learned whatever it is you went way out of your comfort zone for, make sure you celebrate it and be proud of yourself.

Confidence

Confidence requires an optimistic outlook on life, a look on the bright side. We all suffer from lack of confidence at one point or another, especially if we are outside our comfort zones. A wee inner voice creeps into your head and says, "I can't do that," or, "I am not good enough." If we could add up the time spent having doubtful or negative thoughts, I think it would amount to years of our lives. Just think how we could be more productive if all our thoughts were positive and supportive. In my experience, nothing good has ever come from having negative thoughts. It is a form of self-sabotage, an unhealthy cycle designed by the mind to stop you reaching your full potential. The question is: how can we stop ourselves from spiralling downwards?

Firstly, try to focus on what you can do, not what you can't do. Focus on your strengths, focus on what you are good at. Everyone is good at something; you just have to look for it, acknowledge it and build on it. If you can identify something you are good at then you will do it with confidence. Secondly, try some positive affirmations. If you haven't heard of those, they are words or phrases pertinent only to you which you can say over and over, almost like a mantra. You are replacing the negative, unsupportive thoughts with positive and helpful thoughts. This might sound a bit nutty, but it works. I have a set of positive affirmations that I would like to share with you. They are very personal to me and offset the unhelpful thoughts I can have about myself:

I am confident.

I am fearless.

I am proud.

I am worthy.

I am grateful.

When I repeat these words, I can almost feel my breath slowing down, my back straightening and my resolve returning. Spend some time thinking about what your affirmations might be.

Here's another tip: try to *look* confident. That doesn't mean that you strut about the place looking like you can take on the world (although if you do, good for you). What I mean is that an inner calm can also project a level of confidence. I use a technique called the 'inner smile'. I am literally smiling inside and almost as soon as I do this, I can feel a level of calm and inner confidence emerging. Give it a go and see if it works for you.

Finally, I got an excellent piece of advice from my boss. He told me that "knowledge is power". What he was saying was the more knowledge you have about your subject, your workplace, your products, your people, then the more you will be able to communicate with confidence and authority. It is very empowering.

"An investment in knowledge pays the best interest."

Benjamin Franklin

I know from my own experience that all these things work. All the same, to achieve success with anything we have to put the effort in; we can't just expect it to come our way. Above all, if you really believe you can do something, you will do it. Determination is a powerful motivator.

It is worth having a wee word about intuition. Don't be afraid to use it. Our intuition is a gift – our sixth sense. My feeling is that we rely less on our intuition nowadays because we can easily access detailed information on any situation or subject, so our decisions are all based on information. Therefore, it is always worth taking some time out to examine how you really *feel* about a situation before making the big decisions. What's your *gut* feeling? What is it telling you?

Here's a tip that could literally save your life. I told my eighteen-year-old nephew this before he went off travelling to Australia on his own: if something, someone or somewhere does not feel right in your gut, then it probably isn't. Your gut feeling is almost never wrong.

Your Relationship with Money

"Don't think money does everything or you are going to end up doing everything for money."

Voltaire

If you allow money to be the only driver in your life, then it is likely to consume you and feuds over money can damage a relationship in a heartbeat. Usually, people who talk about it all the time and measure other people by how much money they have are the ones who are the most discontent. They never have enough and never will have enough.

Of course, we need money to live and it would be nice to have enough of it to enjoy what life has to offer. Treat your money as a means to an end but also with the respect it deserves. Take the time to understand where it goes. How much are you wasting every month on services you have signed up for and no longer use? What is necessary expenditure and what is unnecessary expenditure? Look at your payslips, your bank statements, your bills and all your outgoings. Keep track of it. I know it is really dull, but it is a necessary evil and could save you a lot of heartache in the long run.

Part 2

A Serving of Wisdom from My Family and Friends

My Family and Friends

Given that I do not have the monopoly on wisdom, I invited my family and friends to provide some wisdom of their own. What advice would they give to my children as they move on to the next phase of their lives? What lessons have they learned that they can pass on?

My family and friends are from different age groups, different walks of life and have all chosen different paths. From Auntie Rosaleen who joined a closed order convent as a teenager – she is now in her eighties – to one of our friends who lives in New York and is a senior director of a global company, to my oldest friend Carole whose career began in the highly competitive world of advertising and who is now an accomplished psychotherapist.

In short, we have all been on a journey, and we are still on one.

And finally, in the hope of encouraging some home cooking once the nest has been flown, I also asked my friends and family to provide a recipe for something they love eating as a family. The recipes are all easy to make and great to eat, but please don't expect precise instructions or sophisticated healthy-eating guidelines. It is simply a collection of tasty food to stop you having too many takeaways!

I hope you enjoy their servings.

First and foremost, some words of wisdom from

Dad

Lorcan is the person I was telling you about earlier – the one I had to learn a lot of lessons to eventually find. He is kind, funny, very hardworking and loves a party!

> *If you live by these lines below, you will not be far off from being the person I would love to be and to be with.*
>
> *Know yourself.*
>
> *Love all.*
>
> *Gain your point by persuasion, not force.*
>
> *Be ready for reconciliation after quarrels.*

Boiled Beef and Carrots

My recipe is one of our in-family jokes. When the kids were small, they would always ask, "What's for tea?" and I would say, "Boiled beef and carrots," as it sounded so plain and unappealing – not something that children would want to eat. I decided to surprise them one day with exactly that – boiled beef and carrots – and it was amazingly well received.

It is always good to have a traditional meal in your repertoire – you never know when the parents might visit!

✗ Ingredients
Serves 4

1.5 kg joint silverside beef or brisket of beef

1tsp light brown sugar
1tsp salt
½ tsp ground black pepper
2 bay leaves
8 cloves
4 large carrots, peeled and cut into chunks
4 sticks celery, trimmed and cut into slices
Vegetables of your choice to serve
Roasted or mashed potatoes to serve

Method

Wash the beef and pat dry, then place in a deep saucepan or casserole dish.
Add the remaining ingredients.
Pour over sufficient water to just cover and bring slowly to the boil.
Cover and simmer gently for about 3 hours or until tender.
To serve, drain the meat and vegetables and place on a warm serving platter.
Remove the string before slicing and discard the bay leaves and cloves.
Carefully pour the cooking juices into a small pan and boil rapidly to reduce to about a third before serving with the meat.
Serve with roasted or mashed potatoes and green beans or any kind of vegetables you like.

Buonissimo!

Auntie Alison & Uncle Martin

Alison is my sister and both Alison and Martin are godparents to my children. We have had many great times together and I am so grateful for her friendship and love and for the joy her children Neil, Craig and Louise have brought me. She is one of the most self-motivated and determined people I know…and she loves a good dance.

> *It is important to remember kindness to the people around you and to have a focus in study, work and play.*

Spag Bol
Don't you just love a good spaghetti bolognese? It's a true staple.

✗ Ingredients
Serves 5

10 slices pancetta or smoked streaky bacon
1 handful rosemary leaves picked and roughly chopped or a tsp dried rosemary
Splash of olive oil
1 large onion, finely chopped
3 cloves garlic, finely chopped
455 g best minced beef
1 glass red wine
1 level tsp dried oregano
1 400 g tin tomatoes
1 200 g tube tomato purée
Sea salt and freshly ground black pepper

455 g dried spaghetti
1 handful fresh basil
2 handfuls grated Parmesan cheese

Method

Preheat the oven to 180°C/350°F, gas mark 4.
In a large hot pan that can go in the oven, fry the pancetta and rosemary in a little olive oil until golden.
Add the onion and garlic and fry for another 3 minutes until softened, before adding the minced beef.
Stir and continue frying for 2–3 minutes before adding the wine.
Reduce slightly, then add the oregano, the tomatoes and the tomato purée.
Season well to taste, bring to the boil and cover with a lid, then place in the preheated oven for an hour and a half.
Towards the end of the cooking time, put your spaghetti into a large pot of boiling salted water until cooked and then drain into a colander.
Just before serving, add some ripped-up basil to the sauce.
Serve with spaghetti and some grated Parmesan cheese.

Auntie Dolly & Uncle Geoff

Dolly is my lovely sister-in-law and my daughter Keira's godmother. She is the best fun – who wouldn't be with a name like Dolly? She loves lunches with her girlfriends, red wine and having amazing holidays with Geoff on their motorbike. She's a legend.

> *You only get one chance at life so live it to the full, laugh a lot and make great memories.*

Ulster Fry

When we visit Dolly in Belfast, she cooks us a full Ulster Fry on a Sunday morning – a full Irish breakfast with all the trimmings. Trips to Belfast would not be the same without it. Everyone needs a full fry-up once in a while. It's a total treat.

✗ Ingredients
Serves 8

(to be honest, you can put anything you like in this but here's what's in ours)

We always start with a fruit salad full of berries, mango, pineapple etc. with Greek yoghurt. Just the job.

Good quality back bacon – work on about 3 slices per person.

Eggs – the quantity depends on what style of eggs you want. For example, fried, scrambled, poached. For scrambled eggs, work on 2 eggs per person.

Potato bread – 2 to 3 slices per person.

Mushrooms – about 500 g or just enough for a spoonful each.

Cherry tomatoes – about 500 g (leftovers of mushrooms, tomatoes and sausage can always be added into pasta the next day).

1 large can baked beans.

Sausages – again, work on about 2 to 3 per person.

Copious amounts of tea and coffee, bread, toast, croissants, Irish wheaten bread.

Fruit juices.

✗ Method – is there one?

The thing about a full Ulster fry is that it is a bit like Christmas dinner. All the components need to be ready and hot at the same time, so it's a juggling act. The trick is to pre-cook as much as you can and then put them in a warm oven to serve when all the other bits are ready. The sausages, bacon, mushrooms, beans and tomatoes can all be pre-cooked and then covered in foil and put in the oven until they are needed. I probably wouldn't cook them too far in advance otherwise they will dry up but perhaps an hour before would be fine.

In the meantime, you can get started on the eggs and the fried bread and once they are ready you can get everything out on the table ready to go.

Auntie Siobhan & Uncle Michael

Michael is Lorcan's brother and lives and works in Belfast with his family. We have had many great dinners around Siobhan and Michael's table. Siobhan is a great cook who loves her Prosecco and her cats! She is kind and funny.

> *Do your absolute best – that is all you can do.*
>
> *Look after yourself before looking after others. It is almost impossible to care for other people if you don't care for yourself. That is sensible, not selfish.*

Malaysian Chicken Curry

A good curry recipe is a must – great at the weekends.

✗ Ingredients
Serves about 8

1 tbsp oil
1 packet Malaysian curry mix (this can be found in most Asian supermarkets)
2 lbs (900 g) chicken breast fillets
2 large onions
1 tin full fat coconut milk
4 cloves garlic
4 medium potatoes
2 chicken stock cubes

1 tsp garam masala
2 tsp lemon juice
2 tsp cornflour if required
Salt and pepper
2 hard-boiled eggs
Basmati rice – allow 65 g per person
Naan bread

✗ Method

Chop the chicken into small bite-sized pieces
Roughly chop the onions.
Chop the potatoes into small cubes.
Crush the garlic.
Heat the oil.
Put the chicken, onions, potatoes, garlic, curry mix and lemon juice in the pot.
Mix the Malaysian curry mix with 300 ml cold water and crumble in the stock cubes. Add to the chicken mix.
Bring to the boil.
Reduce heat and simmer for 20 minutes or until the chicken is tender.
Add the coconut milk.
If the mixture is a bit runny, add 2 tsp of cornflour to thicken.
Add the eggs on top of the curry before serving.
Serve with basmati rice and naan bread.

Fantastic.

Fintan & Linda

Fintan is Lorcan's cousin and one of his best friends. He loves music, a pint or two of Guinness and some good chat.

> *Take charge of your own life – don't rely on someone else to make your life plans for you because they won't. If you rely on luck to improve your life, nothing is likely to change. Learn to adapt to your circumstances and take responsibility to change it yourself.*

Sausage, Celery and Tomato Bake

This sounds like a great meal for a cold day and you can cook it all at once.

✗ Ingredients
Serves 4

4 celery stalks, thickly sliced on the diagonal
2 red onions, quartered
2 garlic cloves, peeled
½ tsp sea salt
½ tsp ground pepper
1 tbsp olive oil
200 g cherry tomatoes
10 thick sausages – any kind you like
Mashed potatoes to serve

✗ Method

Preheat the oven to 200°C/390°F, gas mark 6.

Mix together the celery, onion, tomatoes, garlic, salt, pepper and olive oil in a large bowl to combine all the ingredients.

Once mixed and coated, place them in a roasting tray and lay the sausages on top.

Bake in the oven for 55 minutes.

Turn the sausages and the vegetables once during baking.

Serve with mashed potatoes.

Delicious.

Lesley & William

My cousin Lesley is one of the nicest people I know. She has no side to her; what you see is what you get. She is kind, funny and has a warm and generous spirit.

> *I would tell you to reach for the sky but never forget your roots.*

Lentil Soup

A good, healthy and warming soup is always one to have in your repertoire. You can make a big pot that lasts for a few days.

✗ Ingredients
Serves 4

1 litre stock (ham stock is better but vegetable if you prefer)
2 tbsp vegetable oil
500 g red lentils
2 onions, chopped
4 carrots, grated
1 tin chopped tomatoes (optional)
Thick slices of bread and butter to serve

✗ Method

If you have time and a spare ham hock, then you can make your own stock. If not, just use stock cubes – that's what they are for!

Put the vegetable oil in your soup pot on a low heat.

Add the onions and carrots and cook for 5 to 6 minutes to soften.

Add the lentils and tomatoes if you're using them.

Pour in the stock and cook for about 20 minutes or until all ingredients are fully cooked.

If it is too thick, add more stock until you get the correct consistency.

Serve hot with lots of thick slices of bread and butter.

Great!

Auntie Marie & Uncle John

A devout Roman Catholic, Auntie Marie's faith is the most important thing in her life. Her faith has supported her through thick and thin and she lives her life by the words below.

She took up skiing at the tender age of sixty-five – need I say more?

> *Love God, your family, yourself and your neighbour.*

Sweet and Sour Chicken

The great thing about this recipe is that chicken thighs are less expensive to buy and all the other ingredients are easy to find. You could also substitute the chicken for sausages.

✗ Ingredients
Serves 2

4 chicken thighs – allow 2 per person
4 tbsp tomato ketchup
2 tbsp balsamic vinegar
2 bay leaves
A sprig fresh rosemary or half a tsp dried rosemary
Salt and pepper
2 tbsp sweet and sour sauce (you can buy this in any supermarket)
Serve with rice or couscous and vegetables of your choice

✗ Method

Preheat the oven to 180°C/350°F, gas mark 4.

Season the chicken with salt and pepper, the bay leaf and the rosemary.
Place in an ovenproof dish and cover with foil.
Cook in the oven for one and a half hours.
In the meantime, make the sauce by combining the ketchup, balsamic vinegar and sweet and sour sauce.
Cook the rice or couscous according to the packet instructions.
Prepare and cook any vegetables you want to serve with it.
Remove the chicken from the oven and drain off the fat.
Gently heat the sauce through when the chicken and vegetables are ready.
Pour over the sauce and enjoy.

Auntie Rosaleen

Auntie Rosaleen (Sister Alicia) found her calling as a teenager and joined the Dominican Sisters Convent in Belfast. Her journey took her to Portugal where she spent many years running a school. She has the most beautiful and joyful spirit and radiates love and kindness wherever she goes.

> *My piece of advice is… As you walk through the journey of life remember that God walks with you. Chat to Him, He is your friend. Be the person God wants you to be.*

Victoria Sandwich

Everyone needs to know how to make a basic cake at some stage in their lives. This one will stand you in very good stead.

Ingredients

Serves 6 or 8 depending on how big a slice you want

The quantities for this recipe are easier to remember in old money because you can easily recall the main ingredients of butter, sugar, flour and eggs as 4, 4, 4 and 2.

4 oz butter or margarine
4 oz caster sugar
4 oz plain flour, sieved
2 eggs
¼ tsp baking powder
¼ tsp vanilla essence
2 tbsp strawberry or raspberry jam

For the glazed icing:
4 oz icing sugar
A few tbsp boiling water

To decorate:
Chocolate chips? Sweets? Anything you like.

✗ Method

Grease two 7-inch sandwich tins, dust them with a mixture of equal quantities of caster sugar and flour.

Cream the butter, beat in the sugar and continue to beat until quite creamy.

Add the eggs one at a time, beating until the mixture thickens again before adding the second egg.

Mix in the sieved flour lightly, adding the baking powder with the last addition of flour. Add the vanilla.

Divide the mixture between the tins and spread evenly.

Bake at 180°C/350°F/gas mark 4 for about 20 minutes.

Check if it's ready by piercing the cake; if it comes out clean it's ready.

Cool on a wire tray, spread them with jam while still warm and put together.

Make the glazed icing to the consistency of thick cream with the boiling water and beat well.

Spread the icing on top of the cake and decorate.

Heavenly.

Carole & Jamie

Carole and I became best friends at the age of fourteen. I love her for her fierce intelligence, her razor-sharp wit, her great taste (especially in friends!) and her huge heart. She has been on her own journey of self-development over many years.

We are each of us made of different ingredients.

Look within yourself to see what yours are and you have the beginning of a recipe. Some of the ingredients you might like more than others. The important thing is to have an idea of what they are: the ones you quite like; the ones you like a little less; the ones you decide to focus on and perhaps develop within the recipe to make it the best recipe you can be – knowing it will be worth sharing with others.

My love to you.

Zucchini Pensando

This is a recipe to impress your pals with – even the name is impressive!

✗ Ingredients
Serves 2

2 tbsp olive oil or more if needed

3 courgettes

2 tsp chilli flakes

4 tbsp pine kernels

2 lemons' grated zest – unwaxed, avoiding bitter pith

6 tbsp Parmesan, grated

4 spring onions, finely chopped
1 chicken stock cube for pasta water
1 tsp salt
Enough pasta for 2 people

✗ Method

Grate the courgettes with a coarse grater. Tumble the grated courgettes into a thick tea towel. The tea towel will absorb the excess water after a few minutes.

Put the olive oil in a deep pan.

Add the chilli and spring onions on a low heat for 10 to 12 minutes.

After the chilli and onions have been cooking for about 8 minutes, add the courgettes and increase to a medium heat. If needed, add a bit more olive oil.

At the same time, add the pasta to boiling water with the stock cube and the salt.

Warm the pine nuts in a separate pan on a very low heat for about 10 minutes. Gently shake occasionally to avoid burning.

After 10 minutes, drain the pasta (still al dente) and add to the chilli/onion/courgette mix, adding 2 ladles of the pasta water.

After 3 minutes on a low heat, add one third of the Parmesan and stir slowly.

Sprinkle on the lemon zest and the warmed pine nuts.

Serve in warmed bowls with some of the remaining Parmesan for sprinkling. The pasta should have a little of the remaining pasta water in the base of the serving bowl.

Enjoy xxx

Ann & Al

Ann is one of my besties. She is fabulous, fearless and never afraid to speak up. An entrepreneur always striving to learn new things. She goes out of her way to support young people in business.

Ann's quote for life would be:

> *"If you think you can, you can. If you think you can't, you're right."*
>
> *Henry Ford*

Chicken Risotto

Learning to make a good risotto gives you lots of meal options as you can swap ingredients in and out as you please. It takes about twenty-five minutes to cook.

⚔ Ingredients
Serves 4 or 3 if you want a big plateful!

Splash of virgin olive oil
2–3 chicken breasts, diced
1 medium-sized onion, chopped
200 g risotto rice
1 tub crème fraîche
A handful of frozen peas
4 chicken stock cubes
50 g Parmesan cheese, grated
Ciabatta or garlic bread to serve

✖ Method

Cook the onion gently in the olive oil.

Add the chicken and peas.

Cook on a low heat for around 10 minutes.

Add the chicken stock cubes dissolved in some hot water.

Add the crème fraîche and Parmesan and stir gently for 2–3 minutes, making sure the consistency is fairly fluid (add some water if it's too thick).

Have the rice cooking in a separate pan according to the packet instructions and once cooked, rinse out with hot water to remove excess starch.

Add the rice to the sauce mixture and stir until the rice is fully coated, then serve with either warm crusty ciabatta or garlic bread.

Done.

Laura & Chris

Laura is my other bestie and is an amazingly positive person. She never lets life grind her down and deals with life's challenges with humour and flair.

> *Life isn't a rehearsal, so live life to the full, follow your dreams and treat others as you would like to be treated yourself.*

Granny Simpson's Cake

This recipe was from Laura's grandmother. It has been in her family for over eighty years and is the most comforting cake.

✖ Ingredients
Serves 8

6 oz butter
6 oz sugar
4 eggs, beaten
8 oz plain flour
1½ lbs raisins or sultanas
12 oz glacé cherries
A slug of whisky or brandy

✖ Method

Preheat the oven to 130°C/265°F, gas mark 1.
Grease and line a round 9-inch tin with greaseproof paper.
Beat the butter and sugar till creamy and add the eggs, then the flour a spoonful at a time.

Add the fruit.
Add the whisky or brandy.
Bake for 2 hours.
Check if it is ready by piercing the cake; if it comes out clean it's ready, if not, bake for a little longer until thoroughly cooked in the middle.

Lovely.

Julie & Martin

Julie and I met when we were each expecting our first child and we just clicked. We leaned on each other a lot during those early years of nappies and sleepless nights. Of course, the occasional glass of wine helped. That was seventeen years ago and we are still here for each other.

> *Embrace the mistakes you make and your perceived imperfections.*
>
> *Without mistakes we never learn.*
>
> *Just like the wonky fruit in the recipe below, it's what's on your inside that matters.*

Apple Crumble

Crumble is the simplest and loveliest dessert (it's also great cold for breakfast).

What I love about it is you can use any fruit in season. If the fruit is a bit bashed and wonky shaped, it only adds to the flavour. A great pudding is a wonderful end to a meal.

✗ Ingredients
Serves 4

3 medium apples, peeled, cored and sliced
Squeeze of honey if desired

For the crumble:
175 g plain flour

110 g caster sugar
110 g cold butter

Serve with ice cream, cream or yoghurt.

✗ Method

Heat the oven at 180°C/350°F, gas mark 4.

Lay the fruit in an ovenproof dish. Squeeze over some honey or sugar if you want to make it a little sweeter. I personally love the fruit just as it comes.

Now chop the butter into chunks and mix with the flour and rub it between your fingers until it forms a breadcrumb consistency.

Then add the sugar and mix with a metal spoon to make sure the sugar is evenly spread among the crumbs.

Sprinkle the topping over the fruit.

Cook in the centre of the oven for 30–40 minutes. Then leave for 10 minutes before serving with ice cream, cream, or my favourite, plain yoghurt.

Enjoy!

Cathryn & Paul

When I had the children, a world of new friends opened up to me through schools and clubs, and that's how I met Cathryn and Paul. I love their friendship and admire them for their thoughtfulness, great sense of fun and giant intellect. We've also had some fantastic parties!

Some wisdom from Paul:

> *Don't get hung up on worrying what other people think, as they're too busy worrying what other people are thinking of them.*

Some wisdom from Cathryn:

> *Be kind; be yourself. Listen to others and speak up for yourself. People who belong in your life will come and they will stay.*

Pizza

A Saturday night staple and you can add whatever you like to it. After all, who doesn't like pizza? You'll impress everyone with this one.

✗ Ingredients
Serves 4

10 g yeast sachet
½ tsp sugar
500 g plain flour plus extra for putting on the surface when you knead the dough
1 tsp salt, plus pinch salt
4 tbsp olive oil

1 onion, chopped
2 cloves garlic
440 g tin chopped tomatoes
Squeeze of tomato sauce
1 tsp sugar
375 ml warm water
1 tsp dried herbs (optional)
Grated cheese or mozzarella or any other toppings you like

✗ Method

Make the dough:

Dissolve the yeast sachet into the warm water with the sugar. Leave for 10 minutes until it goes frothy.

Put the flour into a bowl. Add a teaspoon of salt and make a well.

Pour the olive oil into the well with the yeast mixture.

Using a butter knife, mix until it's combined. Then tip the mixture onto a floured surface and knead for 10 minutes until smooth. If you rub oil onto your hands first, the dough won't stick.

Put the dough back in the bowl, cover and leave for at least 45 minutes or until it doubles in size.

If you can't be bothered making your own dough, you can buy frozen pizza bases at the supermarket!

Make the sauce:

Fry the onion and the garlic until they are soft.

Add a pinch of salt then the tin of tomatoes, the tomato sauce, the sugar and some dried herbs if you have them.

Simmer for 30 minutes.

Tip the dough out and flatten. Knead for 5 minutes then divide into four balls (or two if you're hungry!). Roll out with a rolling pin.

Heat the oven to 200°C/390°F, gas mark 6.

Put the bases on a floured tray, add a couple of scoops of sauce, sprinkle with cheese and any other toppings you like. Bake for 10–15 minutes.

Mel & Richard

More friends from baby days – Mel is my coolest friend and has an incredible sense of style. She set up a home-styling business just after her fiftieth birthday.

> *Don't compare yourself with other people – it really doesn't get you anywhere and by the time you realise that the person you thought 'had it all' actually doesn't, you've wasted too much time on it – time that you could have spent having fun!*

Mincey Naan

Make as much mess as you like with this one. Definitely to be enjoyed watching a movie.

✗ Ingredients
Serves 4

Olive oil
500 g mince (lamb or beef)
1 small onion, finely chopped
Spices (cinnamon/cumin/chilli flakes – about half a teaspoon of each)
Salt
Black pepper
2 large naan breads (or 4 minis)
Natural/Greek yoghurt
1 clove garlic
Seeds from a pomegranate

50 g pine nuts (roasted slowly in a warm frying pan. Watch out as they can burn quickly)
Fresh chopped parsley to garnish

✗ Method

Heat a glug of olive oil and fry the onion until lightly golden.
Add the mince and continue to fry until cooked through (squish with a fork to make sure it's cooked).
Now add some spices – it's really up to you what you add but I usually add about a good half teaspoon of cinnamon, cumin and chilli. The more you make it, the more you know how much spice is best for you.
Season with the salt and pepper.
Mix some crushed garlic through a bowl of Greek yoghurt (we have 2 different bowls usually as half the family like a little bit of garlic and the other like it very, very garlicky!).
Warm up the naan and then spread a generous layer of the garlic yoghurt onto the naan. Top generously with the warm mince and then sprinkle with the roasted pine nuts, pomegranate seeds and chopped parsley.

Be warned – it's a very messy dish but totally worth it. We love it.

Richard

(husband of Mel and self-confessed 'better half')

In terms of good advice and opinions on life, I have loads, none of them mine or that original. As a parent I always feel quite inadequate when trying to come up with a silver bullet moment where words of wisdom shine a light on a specific problem. However, I love quotes and I've been given some wise words from others over the years, so here are a few:

Fake it till you make it. I'm still doing that. I think kids today have it hard. We've all done pretty well, be it academically or life partners or career-wise. So, I like to think that the one thing we can do with our kids is to let them know we've been lucky and that it's OK to mess up. So, number one…it's OK not to be perfect – be yourself and do your best. Just turn to the people you love and whom you trust and let them help you to 'get back on the horse' when you think you've failed.

Finally, I genuinely think that kids should know that it's not about what you achieve, or how bright you are, how handsome or how beautiful etc. You can go a long way by just getting on and taking people as you find them.

"It's nice to be important, but it's more important to be nice." However, I would add my own wee bit to that… "It doesn't mean you should take shit from anyone."

Stovies (thanks, Richard's mum)

This is my mum's recipe for 'Stovies'. As a kid, I was never happier than when this was on the table and our family love it now too. The ultimate comfort food.

✗ Ingredients

Serves 4

6 steak slice sausages
1 onion
2 carrots
A small turnip
500 g potatoes
2 beef stock cubes dissolved in water as directed on the packet

✗ Method

Set the oven at 200°C/400°F, gas mark 6.
Cut each sausage into four.
Thinly slice the onion.
Cut the carrot and turnip into approximately inch-size chunks.
Peel and slice the potatoes into 2 cm pieces.
Dissolve the beef cube as directed.
Put it all into an ovenproof pot and half cover with the liquid.
Cover and place in the oven.
Cook for approximately 45 minutes.

Keep checking the pot and testing the potatoes and vegetables. Add more liquid if necessary.

Sheila & Johnnie

Johnnie is one of Lorcan's life-long friends and just the best fun. Both Sheila and Johnnie are into wild swimming – I don't know how they do it!

Sheila's advice:

> *Don't be afraid to be yourself. As you travel along life's journey you will find yourself mixing with lots of different people – at work and/or in education, with your social life and through your chosen leisure pursuits. When you find yourself with new people, it's normal and natural to try and fit in. We all change a little as we do so. There are many different kinds of people in the world, with many different backgrounds. All have value. Accept that you will not like everyone. Accept that not everyone will like you. That's OK.*
>
> *Focus your efforts on spending time with people who gladden your heart and lift you up. When you have to spend time with people who do not, remember that you cannot control how people behave towards you; you can only control how you react.*
>
> *Nobody can make you feel bad without your permission.*

Johnnie's advice:

> *Don't be a bystander. Get on the playing field!*

Roasted Vegetables with Puy Lentils

This dish is super healthy and will impress any vegetarian.

✗ Ingredients
Serves 4

1 pack puy lentils
1 block halloumi cheese
Vegetables for roasting – we use aubergine, red pepper, red onion and courgette. 1 or 2 of each.
Garlic oil – a great substitute for chopping garlic
Balsamic vinegar
Salt and pepper
A jar of salsa

Method

Preheat the oven to 180°C/350°F, gas mark 4.
Chop the vegetables into large chunks or bite-size pieces.
Toss the vegetables into a large bowl with a little of the garlic oil.
Lay out the vegetables on an oven tray, grind over a little pepper and roast for 25 minutes, or a bit longer depending on how you like them.
While the vegetables are roasting, slice the halloumi about 0.5 cm thick.
Grill or fry halloumi for a couple of minutes on each side in a lightly oiled pan.
Make a dressing by mixing 25ml each of garlic oil and balsamic vinegar.
Warm up the puy lentils either in the microwave or in a small pan.
When the vegetables are ready, assemble the dish by layering the lentils first, then the roasted vegetables, then the halloumi on top. Spoon over a little of the salsa for extra flavour.

Relax and enjoy.

Lucy & Barney

Lucy is my creative friend and is a script editor in the TV and film industry. I respect her for her environmental conscience and strong principles. Barney is an entrepreneur and brews his own beer, aptly named Barney's Beer!

> *So, on the advice front, there are two good pieces of advice. The first is for a teen boy who learns to drive – better late in this world than early for the next. I sometimes speak it out loud on my way to work to put things in perspective and stop me driving erratically for the sake of a TV show.*
>
> *The next is let people know when you make a mistake; everyone makes them, and it can only be undone once it is out in the open.*

Bean and Pasta Soup (fantastic for vegans)

Even if you are not a vegan, it is always good to have a vegan recipe to hand and it is delicious.

✗ Ingredients
Serves 4

1 small onion
1 tbsp olive oil
1 clove garlic
2 medium carrots, sliced small or grated
1 stick celery, sliced small
1 tsp mixed herbs

1 tsp oregano
500 ml tomato passata
1 tsp sugar
1 litre vegetable stock, hot
100 g pasta bows
1 tin baked beans
Salt and pepper to season
Hunk of bread or a slice of pizza to serve

Method

Cut the onion up small and fry on a low heat for 5 minutes in the olive oil.

Add the carrots, celery and garlic and fry for another 2 minutes.

Add the herbs for a minute.

Then add the tomato passata, the stock, sugar and pasta. Cover and bring to the boil and cook for 8 minutes on a low heat.

Add the beans, salt and pepper to taste and cook for another 5 minutes, then serve with a hunk of bread or slice of pizza.

Mick & Christie

Mick is Lorcan's oldest friend and has lived and worked in the USA for many years. His successful business career is a result of hard work, continuous self-development and an understanding of how to get the very best out of people. He is generous to a fault.

> *Don't worry about failures (you will have many). They will teach you more about yourself than your successes.*

Barbecue Beef Rolls

This recipe is from the USA and you might find it difficult to get hold of one of the ingredients as the recipe I was given recommends crescent rolls or dinner biscuits. I tried it with frozen Yorkshire puddings, and it worked a treat. This is a fantastic recipe if you want something very easy, tasty and messy. Here we go!

✗ Ingredients
Serves 4

8–10 frozen Yorkshire puddings (instead of crescent rolls or dinner biscuits)
450 g ground beef
About 200 g grated cheese
1 onion, finely chopped
A cup of barbecue sauce

✗ Method

Preheat the oven to 180°C/350°F, gas mark 4.

Brown the onion in a saucepan on a medium heat then add in the beef.

Add the barbecue sauce, stir through, and cook on a medium heat for 10 minutes.

Arrange the Yorkshire puddings onto a baking tray.

Add the ground beef and top with the cheese.

Bake in the oven for 20 minutes.

Let them cool for a minute and then remove them from the baking tray.

Tom & Debbie

Tom was at university with Lorcan and was our best man. He is also godfather to Jack. They recently gave up living and working in the city and to take up farming in Perthshire. They have had many memorable times together.

> *Life is not a dress rehearsal. Don't continue with something that your heart is not set with.*
>
> *Work hard, be kind and get involved.*
>
> *Always question your behaviour, and if it hurts others don't look at them but look at yourself. This will only become more relevant in this intolerant world we are living in.*

Shakshuka

A tasty and nutritious brunch, lunch or light supper. This is SO good.

✗ Ingredients
Serves 4

Olive oil
2 red onions, sliced
2 red peppers, sliced
Sliced chorizo – if using
500 g cherry tomatoes, halved
4 cloves garlic, finely chopped
1 tsp smoked paprika
1 red chilli, finely chopped

80 g spinach
4 eggs
50 g crumbled feta
Chopped parsley
Salt and pepper to season
Crusty bread to serve

✗ Method

Fry the onions in some olive oil until soft, then add the peppers and garlic and cook for 2 minutes.

Add the tomatoes and cook gently until the mixture thickens.

Add the paprika and chilli and cook for 2 minutes.

Stir in the spinach, season and cook until the liquid is reduced.

Make four wells in the mixture and break an egg into each.

Pop on a lid and cook the eggs to your liking.

Sprinkle with the crumbled feta, parsley and a drizzle of olive oil.

This is great served with crusty bread.

Sliced cooking chorizo or whole mini ones can be added at the start with the onions etc. to make the dish meatier and not just a veggie option.

Fantastic.

> Life is not meant to go smoothly. It is full of highs and lows and twists and turns. You will have fantastic days and you will have terrible days and you will have many ordinary ones in between. Be grateful for them all and trust that no matter what life throws at you, you will be able to deal with it.

Chicken Soup

I really do believe that a bowl of soup is good for the soul. If someone is ill in our house, or we are all cold and needing some comforting and nourishing food then chicken soup is something that perks us all up. It is rich in flavour, warming and generally just good for you.

If you have bought a whole chicken and have used all the meat from it, put the carcass into a large pot and add the ingredients below to make a good stock. If you do not have a chicken carcass then use two or three chicken stock cubes in 1½ litres of water.

✗ Ingredients
Serves 4

For the stock:
Chicken carcass
1 onion
1 carrot
1 stick celery
A bay leaf
1 litre boiling water

For the soup:
3 carrots, chopped
1 celery stick, chopped
1 leek, chopped

50 g long grain rice
Salt and pepper
About 150 g cooked chicken, cut into small pieces
Some chopped parsley
Lots of bread and butter to serve

✗ Method

Put all the ingredients into a pot to make the stock.

Bring to the boil and simmer for about an hour.

Pour it all into a sieve and discard the ingredients, leaving the liquid stock.

Once you have the stock you might need to add some boiling water to it in case it is too concentrated.

Add all the chopped vegetables to the stock and simmer for about 45 minutes.

Add the rice and cook for another 15 minutes.

Add more boiling water if you need to.

In the last 5 minutes, add the cooked chicken and some chopped parsley to garnish.

Serve with lots of bread and butter.

Delicious.

Acknowledgements

Thank you to all my family and friends for their inspirational and thoughtful contributions. They all spoke from the heart and their words of wisdom were a true reflection of themselves. I am proud to know them all.

I would also like to thank Judy Turner whom I contacted and asked for her opinion of my initial idea. Judy gave me the encouragement and the confidence to go full steam ahead. Thank you also to my lovely niece Louise, to whom I nervously gave my manuscript. She provided me with lots of positive feedback and some great ideas.

Thank you also to the team at SilverWood Books. You made a newcomer to the world of self-publishing feel like I was in safe hands.

I have greatly enjoyed writing this book. It has taken a huge amount of courage to put myself out there and I have had to keep reminding myself to heed my own advice – that being out of my comfort zone will help me to grow.

Finally, to my husband Lorcan and children Jack and Keira, our two incredible teenage reasons for this book. It would not have been possible without you.

My love to you all.